# The **CB**
# Picture Dictionary

# The CB Picture Dictionary

by Joan Murray

Illustrated by Rose Sommerschield

Doubleday & Company, Inc.
Garden City, New York

For Jimmy, "The Granger Ranger"

Design by Joan Murray

Library of Congress Cataloging in Publication Data

Murray, Joan, 1945-
  The CB picture dictionary.

  SUMMARY: Presents definitions for CB terms.
  1. Citizens band radio—Dictionaries, Juvenile.
[1. Citizens band radio—Dictionaries] I. Sommerschield, Rose. II. Title.
TK6570.C5M87    384.5'3'0321

Library of Congress Catalog Card Number 80-1725
ISBN: 0-385-14782-1 Trade
ISBN: 0-385-14783-X Prebound

# Introduction to CB

Truckers have made up a new language that is fun and easy to learn.
This book will teach you that language so that when you ride in the car
you can say

"There's
**A DRAGGIN' WAGON**
at the **OUTDOOR TV.**"

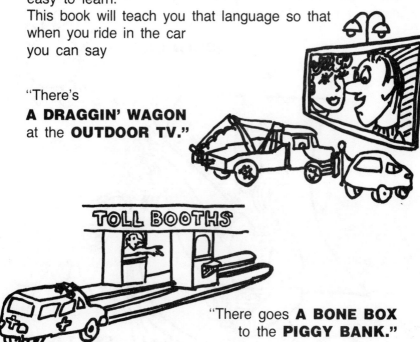

"There goes **A BONE BOX**
to the **PIGGY BANK.**"

Truckers use this language when they talk to other people in trucks or cars on their CB radios.
They call everyone **GOOD BUDDY.**

## Seafarers and Truckers

Long ago seafarers went on long journeys to carry cargo
to distant ports.
Old books show that they had a special language of nicknames for the things they saw:

WORLD CANDLE

WIND NET

SEA TEETH

THE WHALE ROAD

They felt a fellowship with each other, and they told each
other how to avoid dangers on the sea and where to find
safe harbors.

Like the old seafarers, truckers today travel long distances
carrying cargo.
On the highways they talk together in their special language
of nicknames.

**WINDOW WASHER**

**HOLE IN
THE WALL**

CB radios
are like walkie-talkies.

**CONCRETE
JUNGLE**

**TENNIS SHOES**

Truckers have a fellowship too.
They talk on their CB radios to warn of dangers on the
road and help each other find safety and comfort.

## Truck Names

Any truck can be called "**A BUCKET OF BOLTS**," but here are some special names.

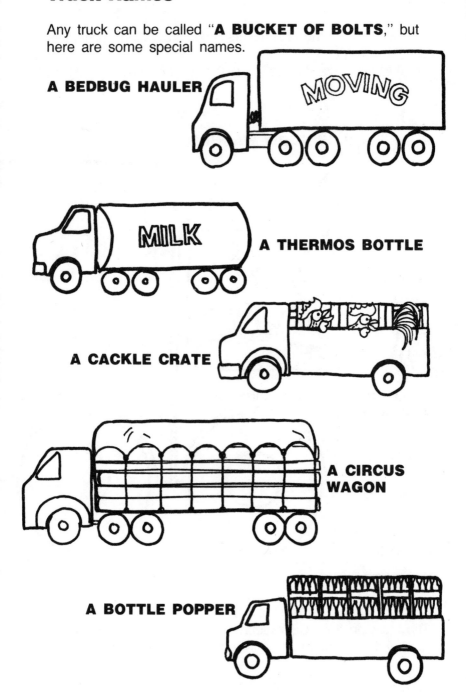

**A BEDBUG HAULER**

**A THERMOS BOTTLE**

**A CACKLE CRATE**

**A CIRCUS WAGON**

**A BOTTLE POPPER**

**A PORTABLE PARKING LOT**

**A PORTABLE FLOOR**

An empty truck carries **A LOAD OF HOLES.**

**A PORTABLE GAS STATION**

An empty tanker carries **A LOAD OF SAILBOAT FUEL.**

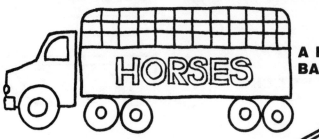

**A PORTABLE BARNYARD**

**A SHANTY SHAKER**

Any truck with a noisy engine is called **A CEMENT MIXER.**

# Here Are More Trucks

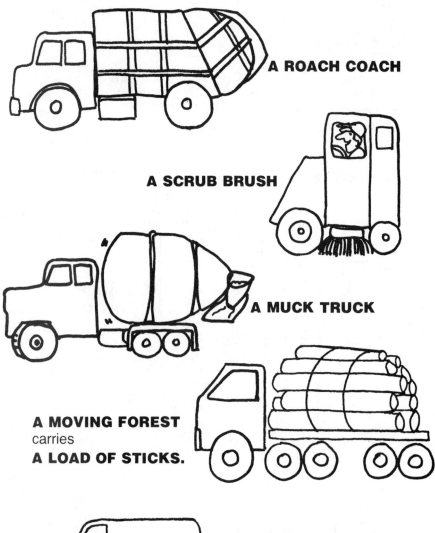

A ROACH COACH

A SCRUB BRUSH

A MUCK TRUCK

A MOVING FOREST
carries
A LOAD OF STICKS.

A DRIVE-IN
DEPOSIT WINDOW

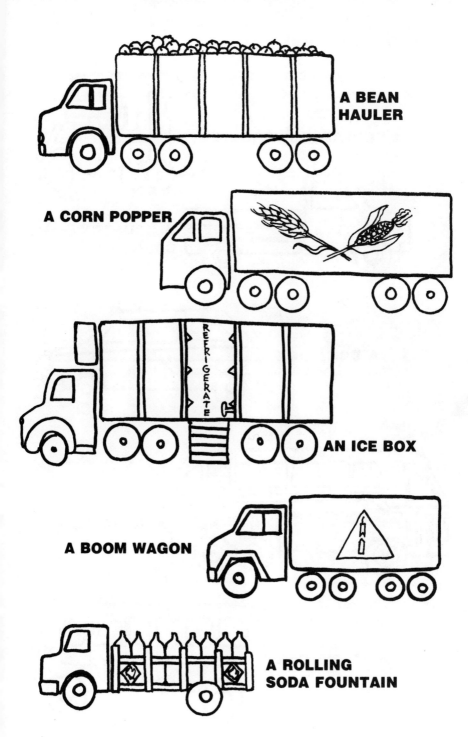

A BEAN
HAULER

A CORN POPPER

AN ICE BOX

A BOOM WAGON

A ROLLING
SODA FOUNTAIN

# Vehicle Names

Here are some other vehicles you'll see on the road.

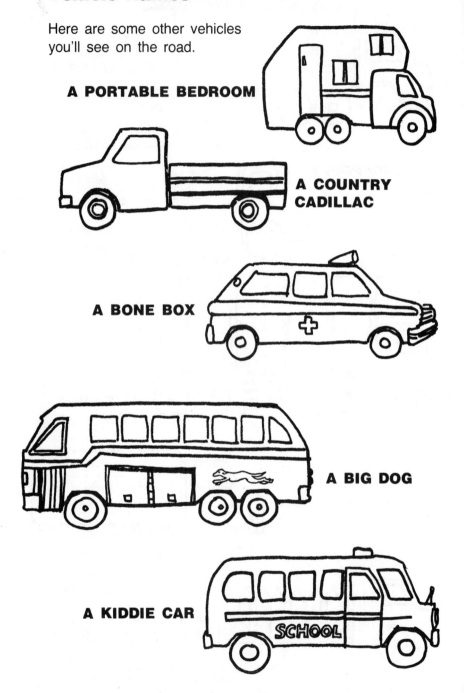

**A PORTABLE BEDROOM**

**A COUNTRY CADILLAC**

**A BONE BOX**

**A BIG DOG**

**A KIDDIE CAR**

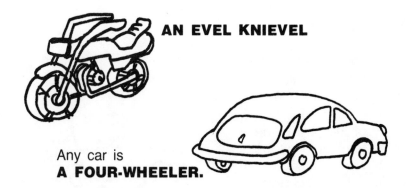

**AN EVEL KNIEVEL**

Any car is
**A FOUR-WHEELER.**

A small car is
**A ROLLER SKATE.**

**A DRAGGIN' WAGON**

**A PIGGY BACK**

**A BELLY-UP**

# The Police

The truckers have many names for the police, who help them when they are in trouble and give  them speeding tickets if they drive too fast.

Many of the police names come from Smokey the Bear, who wears a hat like many police officers or state troopers.

**A BEAR**
or
**A SMOKEY**

**A GIRLIE BEAR**
**A MAMA BEAR** or
**A MAMA SMOKEY**

A rookie
policeman is
**A BABY BEAR**

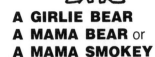

**A BEAR DEN**
or
**A BEAR CAGE**

**BEAR IN THE AIR**
or
**SMOKE CHOPPER**

**TWO-WHEEL SMOKEY**
or
**EVEL KNIEVEL BEAR**

**HAY-BURNING SMOKEY**

**A ROLLING BEAR**
or
**SMOKEY ON SKATES**

If the police car is stopped, **SMOKEY IS DOZING.**

If the police have a
radar speed-reading device,
**SMOKEY'S
TAKING PICTURES.**

Then say **SMILE AND
COMB YOUR HAIR.**

That means "Drive slowly
and carefully and you
won't get a ticket."

But bad drivers get tickets.

**BEAR BAIT**

**SMOKEY DOING
PAPER WORK**

**STARVE THE BEARS** means "Don't get a ticket."

Other names for tickets are: **CHRISTMAS CARDS** or **GREEN STAMPS.**

Here are some other names for police cars:

An unmarked police car is **A BROWN PAPER BAG** or **A PLAIN WRAPPER.**

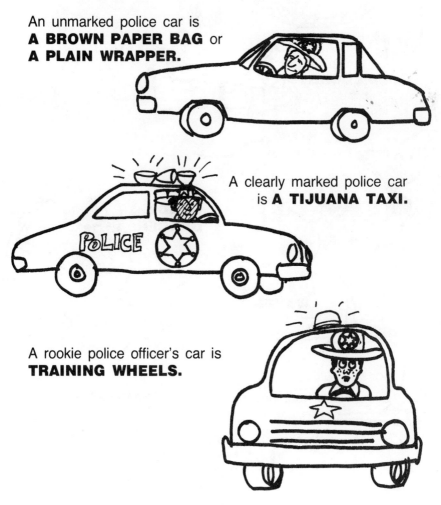

A clearly marked police car is **A TIJUANA TAXI.**

A rookie police officer's car is **TRAINING WHEELS.**

# People on the Road

Some other people the truckers see are

**BUFFALO**

**BUBBLEGUMMERS**

**GOLDILOCKS**

CAUTION CAUTION

**FLAG WAVER**

**GANDY DANCER**

Rush hour drivers are **NINE-TO-FIVERS**

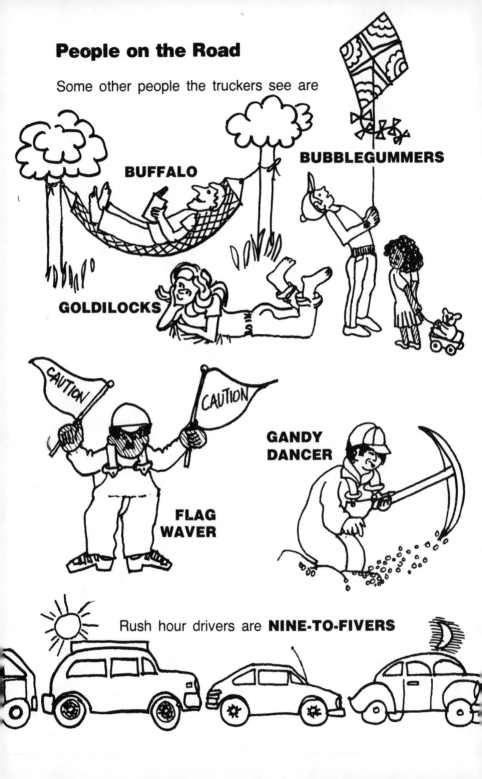

# Bear Bait

### ROGER ROLLERSKATER
Someone who drives
too fast.

### WILLY WEAVER
A drunk driver.

A weaving
car is
**A YO-YO.**

### A BUMPER JUMPER
drives too close.

People who
look at
accidents are
**RUBBER NECKERS.**

### HARVEY WALLBANGER
is a reckless driver.

Here are some other people to look for on the road:

**A SLED HEAD**

**A PEDAL PUSHER**

**WEEKEND WARRIORS**

NATIONAL GUARD

**DANIEL BOONES**

**GARBAGE MEN**

A driver who appears to be lost is called **ALICE IN WONDERLAND.**

**MAN IN A SLICKER**   **MAN IN WHITE**   **MAN IN BLUE**

A parade is called **A WAGON TRAIN.**

# Truckers

Truckers have special names
for truckers too:

Any trucker is
**A PROFESSIONAL**
**A ROAD JOCKEY**
or **A TRUCK-STOP**
**COMMANDO**

A trucker who transports
livestock is
**A BULL HAULER** or
**A SHOAT AND GOAT**
**CONDUCTOR.**

A trucker who hauls
explosives is
**A SUICIDE JOCKEY.**

A trucker's helper is called **A SWAMPER** or **A SHOTGUN.**
(He rides
next to the driver,
just like shotguns
on stagecoaches.)

A beginning
trucker is called
**A WOODCHUCK.**

A trucker who works for different companies is called **A GYPSY** or **A FLOATER.**

A moving van driver is called **A RELOCATION CONSULTANT.**

A driver of a dump truck is called **A DUMP CHUMP.**

A trucking company boss is called **A MUCKETY MUCK.**

# All Along the Road

Snow is **FLUFF STUFF.**

Rain is **WINDOW WASHER.**

Fog is **GROUND CLOUDS.**

A slippery road is **A SKATING RINK.**

The truckers warn each other of these dangers. They also see

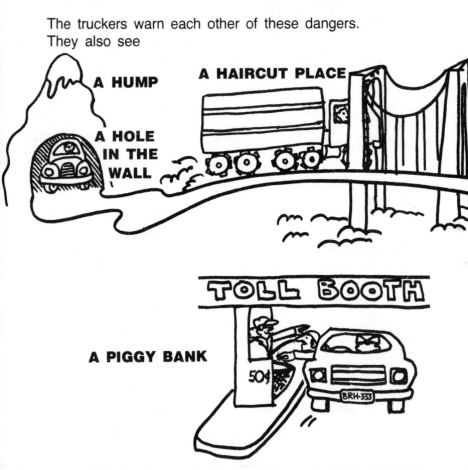

**A HUMP**

**A HOLE IN THE WALL**

**A HAIRCUT PLACE**

**A PIGGY BANK**

TOLL BOOTH

50¢

BRH·333

Truckers can tell each other where to find

**A NAP TRAP**    The trucker is **GETTING SOME Z's** on **THE TRAMPOLINE.**

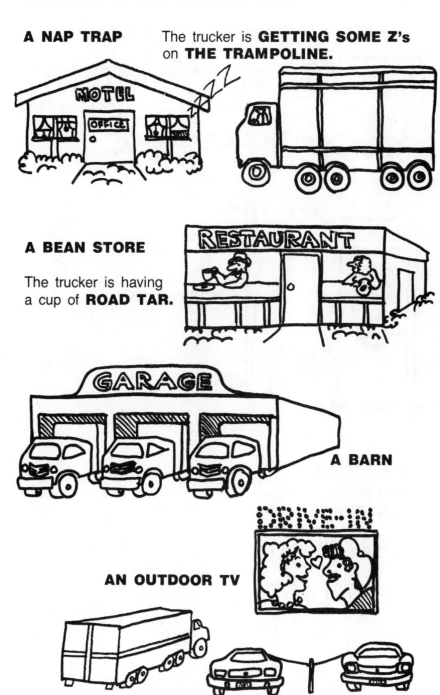

**A BEAN STORE**

The trucker is having a cup of **ROAD TAR.**

**A BARN**

**AN OUTDOOR TV**

You might see these along the road too:

An **OASIS** or **WATERHOLE**

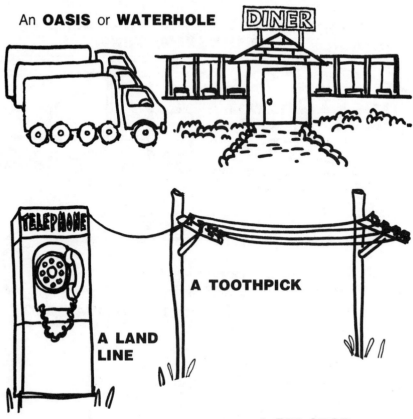

**A LAND LINE**

**A TOOTHPICK**

**A LITTER BOX**

Go here for
**A NATURE BREAK.**

**A PIT STOP**

Go here when your
**SHIP IS SINKING**
(when your vehicle is
almost out of fuel).

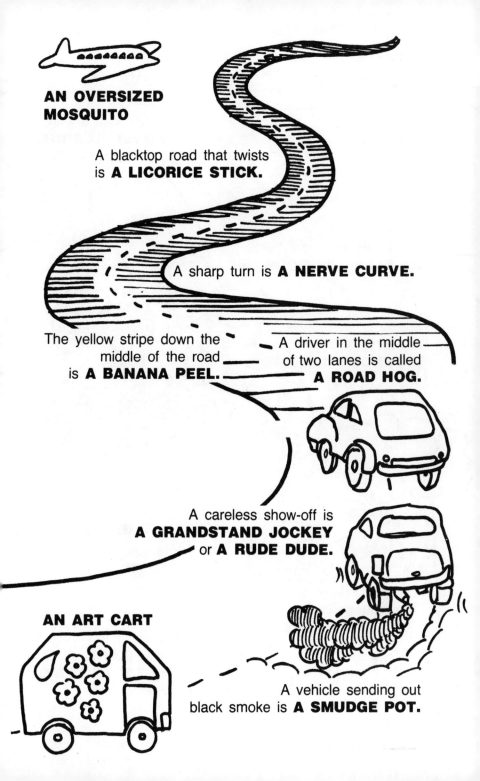

**AN OVERSIZED MOSQUITO**

A blacktop road that twists is **A LICORICE STICK.**

A sharp turn is **A NERVE CURVE.**

The yellow stripe down the middle of the road is **A BANANA PEEL.**

A driver in the middle of two lanes is called **A ROAD HOG.**

A careless show-off is **A GRANDSTAND JOCKEY** or **A RUDE DUDE.**

**AN ART CART**

A vehicle sending out black smoke is **A SMUDGE POT.**

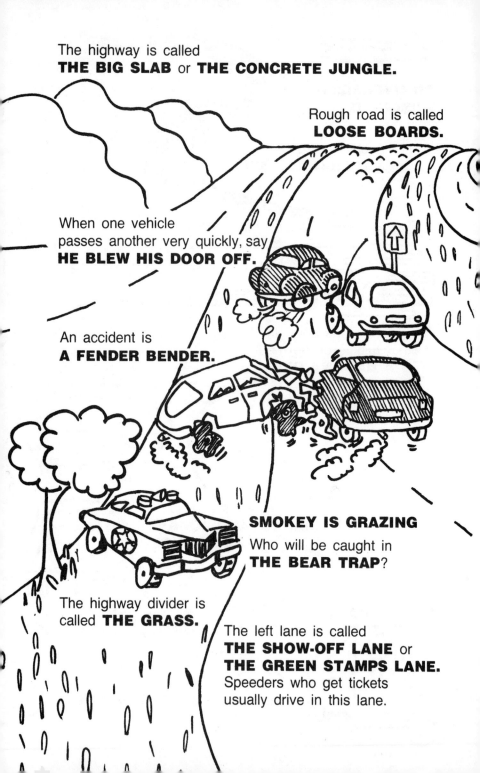

The highway is called
**THE BIG SLAB** or **THE CONCRETE JUNGLE.**

Rough road is called
**LOOSE BOARDS.**

When one vehicle
passes another very quickly, say
**HE BLEW HIS DOOR OFF.**

An accident is
**A FENDER BENDER.**

**SMOKEY IS GRAZING**

Who will be caught in
**THE BEAR TRAP**?

The highway divider is
called **THE GRASS.**

The left lane is called
**THE SHOW-OFF LANE** or
**THE GREEN STAMPS LANE.**
Speeders who get tickets
usually drive in this lane.

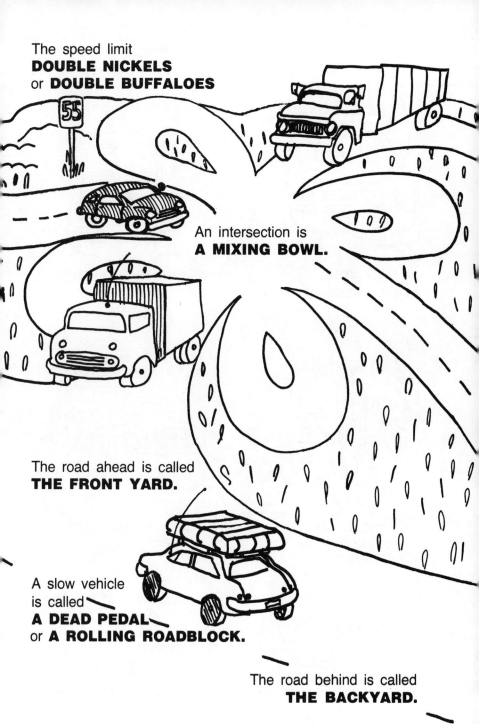

The speed limit
**DOUBLE NICKELS**
or **DOUBLE BUFFALOES**

An intersection is
**A MIXING BOWL.**

The road ahead is called
**THE FRONT YARD.**

A slow vehicle
is called
**A DEAD PEDAL**
or **A ROLLING ROADBLOCK.**

The road behind is called
**THE BACKYARD.**

Have you ever seen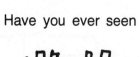

**DARK TIME**
is nighttime.

**A PADIDDLE**
(a car with one headlight)?

**SLEEPIN' PEEPERS**
a car with no headlights)?

Very hard rain is
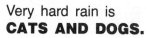
**CATS AND DOGS.**

A flooded road is
**DEEP WATER.**

A construction vehicle is
**A FLAG-WAVER TAXI.**

A detour is
**A BUSTED SIDEWALK.**

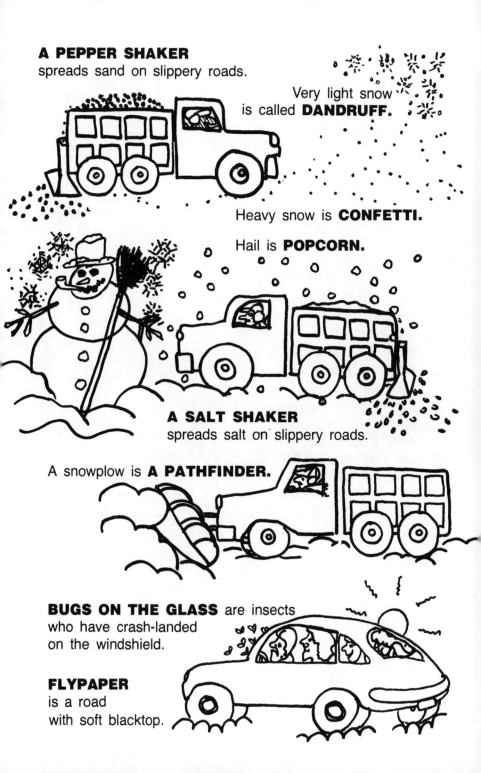

**A PEPPER SHAKER**
spreads sand on slippery roads.

Very light snow
is called **DANDRUFF.**

Heavy snow is **CONFETTI.**

Hail is **POPCORN.**

**A SALT SHAKER**
spreads salt on slippery roads.

A snowplow is **A PATHFINDER.**

**BUGS ON THE GLASS** are insects
who have crash-landed
on the windshield.

**FLYPAPER**
is a road
with soft blacktop.

# Parts of a Truck

The windshield wipers are called **SLAPPERS.**

The mirror is called **A ROLLERSKATE SPOTTER.**

The glove compartment is called **A HIP POCKET.**

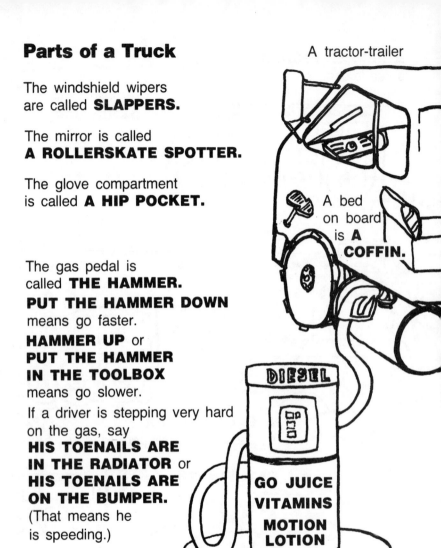

A bed on board is **A COFFIN.**

The gas pedal is called **THE HAMMER.**
**PUT THE HAMMER DOWN** means go faster.

**HAMMER UP** or **PUT THE HAMMER IN THE TOOLBOX** means go slower.

If a driver is stepping very hard on the gas, say **HIS TOENAILS ARE IN THE RADIATOR** or **HIS TOENAILS ARE ON THE BUMPER.**
(That means he is speeding.)

DIESEL

GO JUICE
VITAMINS
MOTION
LOTION

A trucker using the lowest gear is using **THE GRANNY GEAR.**

A trucker using the highest gear has it in **THE GOING-HOME HOLE.**

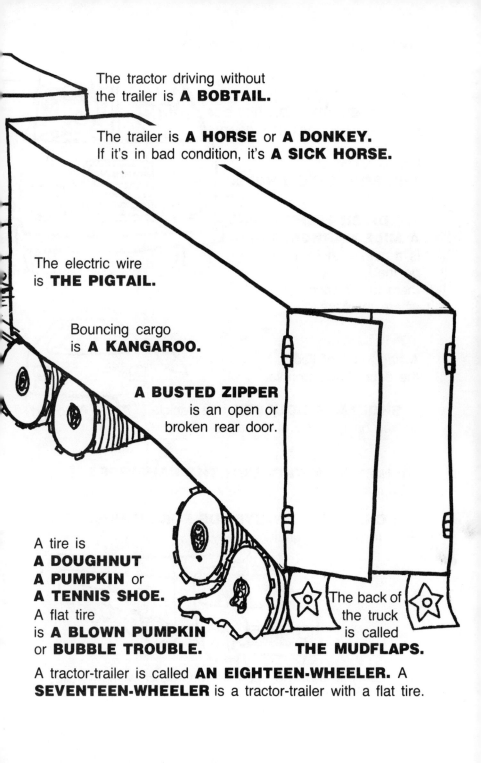

The tractor driving without the trailer is **A BOBTAIL.**

The trailer is **A HORSE** or **A DONKEY.** If it's in bad condition, it's **A SICK HORSE.**

The electric wire is **THE PIGTAIL.**

Bouncing cargo is **A KANGAROO.**

**A BUSTED ZIPPER** is an open or broken rear door.

A tire is
**A DOUGHNUT**
**A PUMPKIN** or
**A TENNIS SHOE.**
A flat tire
is **A BLOWN PUMPKIN**
or **BUBBLE TROUBLE.**

The back of the truck is called **THE MUDFLAPS.**

A tractor-trailer is called **AN EIGHTEEN-WHEELER.** A **SEVENTEEN-WHEELER** is a tractor-trailer with a flat tire.

# Bob the Bean Hauler Makes a Delivery

Benny the Swamper is sitting on **THE BLIND SIDE** (the side that the driver can't look down).

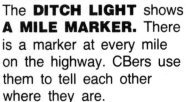

Bob is sitting at **THE ROULETTE WHEEL.**

The **DITCH LIGHT** shows **A MILE MARKER.** There is a marker at every mile on the highway. CBers use them to tell each other where they are.

A handkerchief tied to the door shows trouble.

**A SHOULDER BOULDER** is a vehicle parked on the side of the road.

"I'd like to **RUN THROUGH THE RAINDROPS.**" (Benny means he'd like to take a shower.)

"I'm **CHECKING MY EYELIDS FOR PINHOLES.**" (Bob means he's getting sleepy.)

The terminal is at the 225-mile marker. How many miles must Bob drive?

# At the Terminal

**THE DOCK WALLOPER** unloads the cargo.

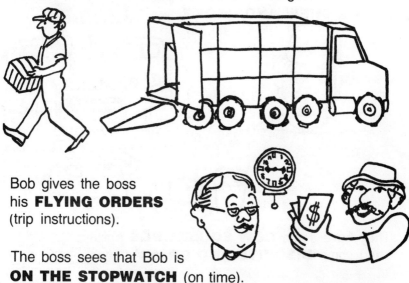

Bob gives the boss his **FLYING ORDERS** (trip instructions).

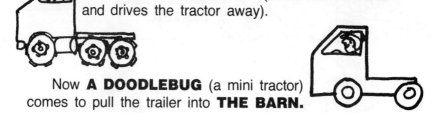

The boss sees that Bob is **ON THE STOPWATCH** (on time). The boss gives Bob some **LETTUCE** or **BREAD** (money).

Bob **DROPS THE BODY** (detaches the trailer and drives the tractor away).

Now **A DOODLEBUG** (a mini tractor) comes to pull the trailer into **THE BARN.**

Bob needs **A CHECK-UP.** Pick 2 to work on Bob's engine:

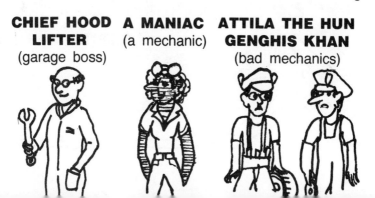

**CHIEF HOOD LIFTER** (garage boss)  **A MANIAC** (a mechanic)  **ATTILA THE HUN GENGHIS KHAN** (bad mechanics)

Bob and Benny go to **THE BEAN STORE.**
"Let's **PUT ON THE FEEDBAG.**" ("Let's eat.")

Here's a **CHEW AND CHOKE** (a restaurant).

They have some **COW SQUEEZINGS** (milk) and some **BISCUITS AND GRAVY** (food).

Then they go to get a room at the **NAP TRAP.**

Bob is watching **THE ONE-EYED MONSTER.**

Benny is in **THE RAIN LOCKER.**

Later Benny goes **GUTTER-BALLING.**

After bowling Benny **LOGS SOME Z's.**

A water bed is **A WAVE MAKER.**

Bob uses the **DOUBLE L** or **LAND LINE** to phone his family.

He talks into the **TWISTED PAIR.**

He talks to his **BETTER HALF** (his wife).

and his **ANKLE BITER** (his bratty child).

He tells them he's taking his **BACKSTROKE** or **BOUNCE AROUND** (his return trip) in the morning.

Bob **HITS THE SNORE SHELF,** but two men having a **KNUCKLE BUSTER** keep him awake.

In the morning Bob and Benny start **PEDALING** again. They are riding empty, **CARRYING A LOAD OF STREAKERS' UNIFORMS.**

# All About CB

CB radios are called
**SQUAWK BOXES**
or **HILLBILLY OPERA HOUSES.**

The microphone
is called
**A LOLLIPOP.**

Antennas are called
**FISHING POLES.**

Two antennas are
**A FISHING POLE AND A**  **PARTNER.**

**A SNOOPERSCOPE**
is a very tall
CB antenna.

**A BALLET DANCER**
is an antenna that
sways in the wind.

**A CHOP TOP**
is a short
CB antenna.

**A CHROME DOME** is an antenna on a four-wheeler.

**A PORCUPINE** is a vehicle with many antennas.

A CB in any vehicle is **A MOBILE RIG.**

A CB in a building is **A BASE STATION.**

A base station with many fishing poles is **AN ANTENNA FARM.**

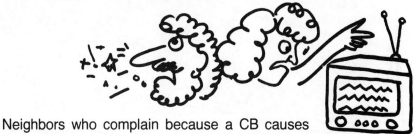

Neighbors who complain because a CB causes TV interference (**TVI**) are the **TENNESSEE VALLEY INDIANS.**

# A CB Convoy

When a group of CBers are traveling the same road in the same direction, they form a band called **A CONVOY.** They talk together on their CB radios and tell each other what is ahead or coming from behind.

The **FRONT DOOR** is the first vehicle in the convoy.

He **SHAKES THE BUSHES**— he checks the road ahead and warns the others.

"Good buddies, there's **WINDOW WASHER** in the front yard."

**A RUMBLE SEAT** is a vehicle without a CB that closely follows a vehicle with a CB.

**PEANUT BUTTER EARS**

is a CBer who doesn't listen carefully.

An experienced CBer is a **BTO** (Big Time Operator).

A conversation of three or more CBers is called **A ROUNDTABLE.**

Any CB operator is called **A BREAKER.** An inexperienced CBer is **A GREEN APPLE.**

Vehicles in the middle of a convoy are **IN THE ROCKING CHAIR.** They can take it easy because they have lookouts ahead and behind.

**THE BACK DOOR** is the last vehicle in a convoy. He **RAKES THE LEAVES**— he reports on vehicles coming from behind.

"Good buddies, a Roger Rollerskater is coming from the backyard."

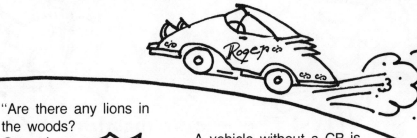

"Are there any lions in the woods? Oops, I mean **BEARS IN THE GRASS**?"

A vehicle without a CB is **RUNNING BAREBACK.**

**A LADY BREAKER**

**A BUBBLEGUM BREAKER**

# CB Means Citizen Band

Truckers have names for some of the citizens who use CB's.

**AN ACE** is an important CBer.

**A CRADLE BABY** is a CBer who is afraid to talk.

**A HAMSTER** is a CBer who hams it up or clowns around on the air.

**BOAST TOASTIES** is a CB expert.

**A TEAR JERKER** is a CBer who tells sad stories.

**A SUNBEAM** or **A FOG LIFTER** is a CBer with cheery or interesting conversation.

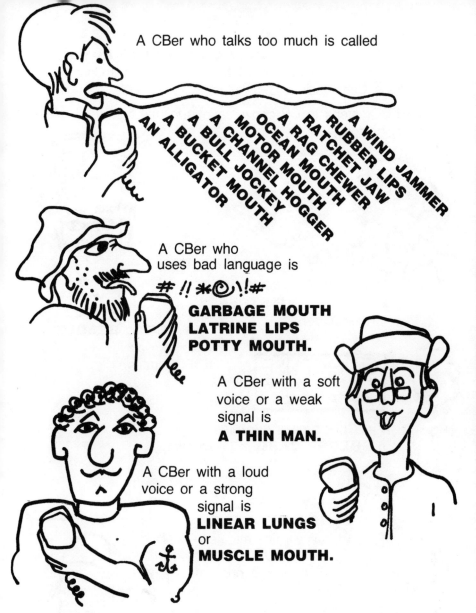

A CBer who talks too much is called

A WIND JAMMER
A RUBBER LIPS
A RATCHET JAW
A RAG CHEWER
AN OCEAN MOUTH
A MOTOR MOUTH
A CHANNEL HOGGER
A BULL JOCKEY
A BUCKET MOUTH
AN ALLIGATOR

A CBer who uses bad language is

# !! *©)\!#

**GARBAGE MOUTH
LATRINE LIPS
POTTY MOUTH.**

A CBer with a soft voice or a weak signal is

**A THIN MAN.**

A CBer with a loud voice or a strong signal is

**LINEAR LUNGS**
or
**MUSCLE MOUTH.**

It is illegal to talk too long on a CB, or to use bad words on a CB, or to use a linear amplifier (a device to make your message go louder and farther).

Who will catch these bad CBers?

The FCC or **THE FRIENDLY CANDY COMPANY** or **FRIENDLY COUSIN CHARLIE** is the Federal Communications Commission.

The FCC listens to CB conversations to make sure all rules are being followed.

**CHARLIE** is **MONITORING. PANIC IN THE STREETS** for bad CBers.

**A LEGAL BEAGLE** follows all the FCC rules.

If a CBer breaks the rules, his **GLORY CARD** is taken away.

**MY NICKEL IS UP.** The FCC allows five minutes—**A NICKEL'S WORTH**—of talking at one time.

**A RENEGADE** is a CBer with no license.

## DESPAIR BOX
is CB parts.

## A BLESSED EVENT
is a new CB set.

## A BAG OF BONES
is a used CB set.

CBers make up nicknames for themselves too. The nick-names are called **HANDLES.** They use their handles when they talk on their CB radios.

"I'm Rubber Ducky."

"I'm Peach Cake."

"I'm Cherry Lips."

"I'm Screaming Eagle."

"I'm Shooting Star."

"I'm Wildcat."

Make up a handle for yourself.  Now you're ready to talk on the air.

**MODULATING** or **JAW JACKING** is talking on the CB.

On the **KEYBOARD** of the CB, **PICK A CLEAN ONE** (find a channel with no one talking on it).

Then **KEY THE MIKE** (push in the button and speak).

If you want to talk to any CBer, make a **GRAB BAG** to anyone who is listening.

**"GOT ANY BREAKERS?"** means "Is there anyone there who wants to talk?"

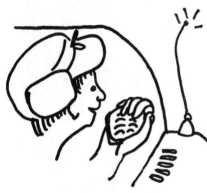

If you see a CBer (look for an antenna) and would like to make contact, say **"YOU IN THE RED FOUR-WHEELER, HAVE YOU GOT YOUR EARS ON?"** That means "Are you listening?"

If you wish to speak to a specific CBer who is in the area, make a **COLLECT CALL** using his or her handle: **"BREAK FOR** Cell Block Bill."

He will answer, "You got Cell Block Bill **BACK AT YA."**

If you want to be sure you are reaching someone, ask, **"YOU GOT A COPY ON ME?"** or **"DO YOU HAVE A COPY?"** That means "Can you hear and understand me?"

If you are receiving a clear, strong signal, answer:

"It's **WALL TO WALL AND TREETOP TALL**!"

"It's **BREAKING THE OLD NEEDLE**!"

"It's **BENDING MY WINDOWS**!"

"It's **COMING IN LOUD AND PROUD**!"

"It's **BENDING THE TREETOPS**!"

"It's **BODACIOUS**!" (It's very good.)

If there is static, say, "We've got **MIKE DUST.**"

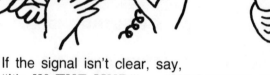

If the signal isn't clear, say, "It's **IN THE MUD**!" or **"NEGATIVE COPY."**

Quickly turning the dial past all the channels is **A QUICK TRIP AROUND THE HORN.**

If all the channels are occupied, **EVERYBODY'S WALKING THE DOG.**

# Marge Uses Her CB for the First Time

First Marge has **MIKE FRIGHT** (she is afraid to speak).

So she just **COPIES THE MAIL** (listens to others' CB conversations).

Then Marge sees **FIREWORKS** (lights from police cars in the distance). She wants to know if there is danger ahead.

She says **"BREAKER BREAKER."** That means she wants to break in and talk.

**"HAVE I GOT A WESTBOUNDER?"**
She wants someone coming from the lights.
**"GO AHEAD. YOU'VE GOT A WESTBOUNDER,"** a CBer says.
**"WHAT ARE THOSE FIREWORKS OVER YOUR SHOULDER?"** Marge asks.
**"THERE BE SOME BEARS WEARING PARTY HATS. THEY WERE MAKING LIKE BUCK ROGERS AND CAUGHT A ROGER ROLLERSKATER."**
(He means there are police cars with their lights on. They were using radar guns and caught a speeder.)

**"THANK YOU, GOOD BUDDY,"** Marge says.

The CBer asks Marge,
**"WHAT ARE YOU PUSHING?"**
She answers,
"A blue **COUNTRY CADILLAC.**"
**"WHO DO YOU PULL FOR?"** he asks.
"Guy's Engine Company," she says.
The CBer says he's in a yellow microbus
and he pulls for Ernie's Produce.

When Marge and the CBer pass they have **A MOBILE EYEBALL.** Marge keeps listening to the CBer as he drives far away. She hears him talking to **A GHOST,** a CBer who is too far away for her to hear at all.

Marge passes a **THUMBSUCKER** (a hitchhiker). His car is disabled.

Marge calls for someone to come and help him. She is **A TALKING LIFESAVER.**

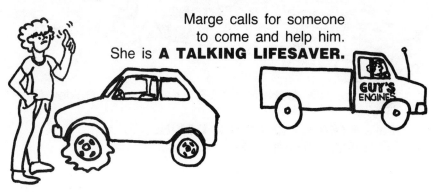

Marge gets a call from another westbounder.
"You've got Golden Glory," the CBer says. "What's your handle?"
"You've got the Iron Maiden," Marge answers.

"How's your backyard?" Marge asks.
"We be in an **ULCER GULCH**" (traffic jam).
"But the eastbound is clean, bring on your machine."

"Someone's **BRUISING MY BODY.** Someone's **STEPPING ON ME**," Marge says.
(That means "Someone's interrupting.")

"Sounds like **WE'RE IN YOUNGVILLE.** I'll **CHECK THE SEAT COVERS**," Golden Glory says.
(That means "Sounds like children are using the CB. I'll look at the car behind me.")

"There be two **ANKLE-BITERS** behind me," Golden Glory says.
"Let's **STEP UP OR STEP DOWN.**
("Let's find a higher or lower channel.")

"I'm **ON THE FLIP-FLOP** from California," Marge says.

"I'm coming from **THE SALT MINES,**" Golden Glory says.
(She means she's coming from work.)

After Golden Glory gets past the traffic jam, she says:
"I'm one foot on the floor, one hanging out the door, and
she just won't do no more." (She means she's traveling at
top speed.)

"You'd better **PULL IN THE REINS,**"
Marge warns, "or you'll be **A PIGEON.**"

(That means "Slow down or
you'll be a vehicle caught for
speeding.")

"That's **BODACIOUS** advice!"
Golden Glory says.

"Time to **TIE THE RIBBONS,**" Marge says.
(That means "Time to end our conversation.")

Truckers have nicknames for many cities. Here are fifteen of them. Can you guess their real names?

HINTS:

1. Boston baked beans
2. New York Apples tennis team
3. The song "Chattanooga Choo-Choo"
4. "Have a Tampa" cigar band
5. The Houston Astrodome
6. San Francisco Bay
7. The glitter of Hollywood
8. The Gateway Arch in St. Louis
9. Las Vegas gambling games
10. Chicago, on windy Lake Michigan
11. Salt Lake City, on the Great Salt Lake
12. Detroit, center of the auto industry
13. Mount Hood near Portland
14. A Butte sound-alike
15. Denver, high up in the Rocky Mountains

You can make up a name for your city just as the truckers do. If you live in Smithville, for instance, where there is a big zoo, you can call it "That Smithville Town" or "big S" or "Zoo City".

In CB talk, your **TWENTY** means your location.
Your **HOME TWENTY** means where you live.

"My **TWENTY** is 'Shaky Town.'"
"My **HOME TWENTY** is 'BEAN TOWN.'"

Here are more CB place names. Can you guess why they got these nicknames?
(If you can't, ask a parent or a teacher or a trucker.)

| | |
|---|---|
| Anchorage, Alaska | "The Iceberg" |
| Atlantic City, New Jersey | "The Boardwalk" |
| Akron, Ohio | "Rubber City" |
| Bismarck, North Dakota | "Battleship City" |
| Boise, Idaho | "Spud Town" |
| Buffalo, New York | "Nickel City" |
| Butte, Montana | "Beauty City" |
| Birmingham, Alabama | "Steel Town South" |
| Casper, Wyoming | "Ghost Town" |
| Charleston, South Carolina | "Charlie" |
| Cheyenne, Wyoming | "Rodeo Town" |
| Disneyland, California | "Cinderella One" |
| Disneyworld, Florida | "Cinderella Two" |
| El Paso, Texas | "Taco City" |
| Flagstaff, Arizona | "Flag Town" |
| Fort Lauderdale, Florida | "Beach City" |
| Fort Worth, Texas | "Cow Town" |
| Grand Rapids, Michigan | "Chair City" |
| Hartford, Connecticut | "Stag Town" |
| Hot Springs, Arkansas | "Hot Water City" |
| Indianapolis, Indiana | "500 City" |
| Little Rock, Arkansas | "Rock City" |
| Long Island, New York | "Shark City" |
| Los Angeles, California | "Shaky Town" |
| Louisville, Kentucky | "Derby City" |

| | | |
|---|---|---|
| Milwaukee, Wisconsin | "Beer Town" |  |
| Minneapolis, Minnesota | "Big Twin" | |
| Montgomery, Alabama | "Monkey City" | |
| Nashville, Tennessee | "Guitar City" | |
| New Orleans, Louisiana | "Mardi Gras Town" | |
| Nome, Alaska | "Troll Town" | |
| Norfolk, Virginia | "Sailor City" | |
| Oklahoma City, Oklahoma | "Oil City" | |
| Philadelphia, Pennsylvania | "Liberty City" |  |
| Phoenix, Arizona | "Sun City" | |
| Roswell, New Mexico | "Cactus Patch" | |
| San Antonio, Texas | "Alamo City" | |
| Seattle, Washington | "Needle City" |  |
| Shreveport, Louisiana | "Sport City" | |
| South Bend, Indiana | "Fightin' Irish Town" | |
| Toledo, Ohio | "Scale City" | |
| Winston-Salem, North Carolina | "Tobacco City" | |

(Some cities have four or five nicknames, so if you listen to CB, you might learn even more.)

Truckers have names for many states, too: Arkansas is "Hog Country." Florida is "The Bikini State." Montana is "The Big Sky." Rhode Island is "The Mini State."

Many states' names are the same as license plate slogans:
Pennsylvania is "The Keystone State."
New Jersey is "The Garden State."
(I asked a trucker for the nickname for Hawaii. He said, "When my truck reaches the Pacific Ocean, she just won't go farther. Call it 'The Aloha State.'")

## Sam and Henry Go to a Moth Ball
## (a Big CB Convention)

Sam and Henry are **TOOLING DOWN THE ROAD** (driving normally).
Then Sam says:
"Either I'm on **A WASHBOARD** (a bumpy road) or this **KIDNEY BUSTIN' VIBRATOR** (truck) has **A SORE FOOT** (a flat)."

"I'm in **THE DOUBLE-JOINTED CORNFLAKES BOX** that's **HOLDING ONTO YOUR MUD FLAPS** (driving right behind you)," Henry says.

"I'd better **DROP IT OFF THE SHOULDER** (pull over) and **KICK THE DONUTS** (check the tires)."

"It's **A SORE FOOT.** Need some help?"

"I'm going to **DUCK OUT** (leave the trailer) and fix it tomorrow. I don't want to be late for the Ball!"

Sam **CLOSES THE GATES** (locks the truck).

Then he drives away **NAKED.**

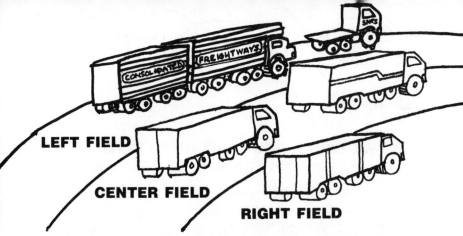

**LEFT FIELD**

**CENTER FIELD**

**RIGHT FIELD**

The road is filled with CBers on the way to the Moth Ball.
Sam says, "**BETTER CRISSCROSS** (change lanes) be-
cause we have to **HANG A RIGHT** (turn right)."
**HANG A LUEY** is a left turn. **HANG A UEY** is a U-turn.

At the Moth Ball Sam and Henry meet **THE GLORY
ROLL** (CBers who are known all over the country).

There are people
selling **GOODIES**

and live enter-
tainment.

(To learn two CB songs,
turn the page.)

## CB Songs

### HERE WE TRUCK DOWN THE INTERSTATE
(Sing to the tune of "Here We Go Round the Mulberry Bush.")

Here we truck down the interstate, the interstate, the interstate,
Not speeding like Roger Rollerskate,
Good buddies, with our ears on.

We'll listen to our big front door, big front door, big front door,
And won't put our hammers to the floor,
Good buddies, with our ears on.

We'll wheel on easy in the rocking chair, rocking chair, rocking
   chair,
'Cause our back door spotted smoke in the air,
Good buddies, with our ears on.

When the window washer starts to fall, starts to fall, starts to fall,
we'll stay dry in a hole in the wall,
Good buddies, with our ears on.

If we need a nap at the end of day, end of day, end of day,
Some other road jockey will show the way,
Good buddies, with our ears on.

Then we'll say adios to our CB friends, CB friends, CB friends,
On the interstate, we'll catch you again,
Good buddies, with our ears on.

## ALL GOOD BUDDIES

(Sing to the tune of "Camptown Races.")

All good buddies sing this song, do da, do da.
Concrete jungle's rough and long, oh the do da day.

> Gonna wheel all night, gonna wheel all day.
> Gonna jack my jaw with CB talk 'cause I know what to say.

I'll put some go juice in my tank, do da, do da.
And pay my toll at the piggy bank, oh the do da day.

> Gonna wheel, etc.

I'll shake them bushes while I pass, do da, do da.
And spot the Smokeys in the grass, oh the do da day.

> Gonna wheel, etc.

I won't put down my hammer hard, do da, do da.
'Cause I don't want a Christmas card, oh the do da day.

> Gonna wheel, etc.

If the road becomes a skating rink, do da, do da.
I'll stop and get some tar to drink, oh the do da day.

> Gonna wheel, etc.

I'll cross a bridge and cut my hair, do da, do da.
Then I'll tuck myself in the rocking chair, oh the do da day.

Gonna wheel all night, gonna wheel all day.
Gonna jack my jaw with CB talk 'cause I know what to say.

# JAW JACK

Here's more **JAW JACK** you can use:

Yes = **AFFIRMATIVE**
No = **NEGATORY**
Drive Safely = **TRUCK 'EM EASY**

Don't do that = **DDT**
Look at that = **LAY AN EYEBALL ON**

**MERCY SAKES** is what truckers say
when they are surprised or angry.
They never use bad words.

Remember:
**JAW JACKING** is
the CB phrase for
talking.

**JAW HACKING** is
talking too much.

# A FEW LAST WORDS

**10-7** Leaving the air)
**10-3** (Stop transmitting)
**73** (Best regards)
**GBY** (God bless you)

**IT'S CUT-OUT TIME**

**GIVE ME A HOLLER AGAIN**
(Call me on the CB another day)

**88s AROUND THE HOUSE** (Good luck to all in your family)

**KEEP THE GREASY SIDE DOWN
AND THE SHINY SIDE UP**
(Don't be a belly-up)

**KEEP THE BUGS OFF THE GLASS
AND THE BEARS
OFF YOUR TAIL**

**88** (Love and kisses)

**HOME FREE**
(Get home safely)

**KEEP YOUR NOSE BETWEEN THE DITCHES
AND SMOKEY OUT OF YOUR BRITCHES**

**STAY BETWEEN THE JUMPS AND BUMPS
AND TRUCK EASY OVER THE HUMPS**

**LET THE CHANNELS ROLL**
(Let others talk now)

**TIME TO PULL THE PLUG**

# A Long So Long

Truckers never say good-bye.

Instead, when they are ready
to leave the convoy they say:

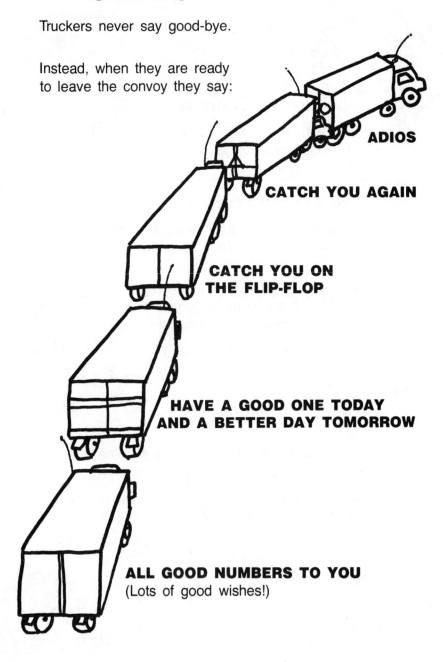

**ADIOS**

**CATCH YOU AGAIN**

**CATCH YOU ON
THE FLIP-FLOP**

**HAVE A GOOD ONE TODAY
AND A BETTER DAY TOMORROW**

**ALL GOOD NUMBERS TO YOU**
(Lots of good wishes!)